Thought Notebook Literary & Visual Art Journal
Issue One
There Is A First For Everything

EDITOR & CREATIVE DIRECTOR - Kat Lahr
ASSISTANT EDITOR - Tom Lahr
ASSISTANT DESIGNER - Destiny Adamski

Published By Thought Collection Publishing

www.thoughtcollection.org
www.thoughtnotebook.org

ON THE COVER
Young Love Is In The Air
by Melody Croft

ISSN: 2334-1572
ISBN-10: 0996663533
ISBN-13: 978-0-9966635-3-3

•• Contents ••

Groups of different thoughts on the Firsts in our lives.

There Is A First For Everything

Conceptual

Ideas conceived in the mind.

Expression

A manifestation of a disposition.

Discovery

Experience allows the ability to form reactions and learn.

IN EVERY ISSUE

Precedent

Welcome to our first issue of *Thought Notebook*, the Literary and Visual Art Journal for *Thought Collection Publishing*. We are thrilled to bring to you a broad range of art from contributors who have partnered with us to build a community in celebration for the arts. This is a first for me and our Publishing Company, thus the inspiration for the theme of the issue – Firsts. At first, we really didn't know what to expect when engaging in a firsts theme, as firsts cover a wide range of topics, yet I am absolutely amazed by the diversity of thought, talent and art that was submitted.

Having or being a part of a first indicates order, coming before, setting a precedence when the experience is recollected in the future. Aren't we all excited to try something we haven't done before? We are living a life full of first experiences, from a first kiss, to the first time giving blood, to conceptual and philosophical explanations of humanity's firsts.

This issue is dedicated to family, the first of all firsts that we are born into. It gives us our name, defines our environment and stamps the starting point for our life journeys, who we meet and who we love. It sets the groundwork for our consciousness and the thoughts that form in our minds. It creates relationships, allowing the medium to experience love and pain. Within the pages of this issue are the stories that come from these foundations.

The pieces in this journal all come from a range of artistic techniques, the diversity of that which is art. Yet underlying similarities come forth. *Thought Notebook's* columns are an output of the thought patterns that arose from the 'firsts' theme. In recording into the notebook these real stories of life and the thoughts we generate about them, we get a glimpse into understanding a great deal about ourselves and society, where our conscious has been and the direction its going. *Thought Notebook* is based on a true story, humanity's story. Our journal documents the expression of our thoughts, deriving from reflection and expanded consciousness.

It is my hope that in this issue you enjoy reading and viewing the literary and visual art depicting life's firsts. We hope to create conversation and community through the openness that defines *Thought Notebook.*

Cheers,

Kat Lahr

Kat Lahr
Editor and Creative Director
Thought Collection Publishing

CONTACT ME

Follow me @thoughtnotebook

Become a fan at facebook.com/thoughtcollection

Growth

**Moments of development
and maturity.**

True Liars Believe The Lies They Tell

Brianne McDonald

> Realizing for the first time, the true and self destructive consequences of our actions.

The day I realized I was a liar I had just narrowly avoided being caught by his girlfriend at their home with my pants down. It was more like a bucket of cold water than being brained by an apple, but the effect was similar. Eureka!

This particular epiphany was followed closely by the realization that I was a bad person. A big one. I'm not sure how I was able to operate under the assumption of moral 'goodness' for so long when all fingers pointed in the opposite direction, but it certainly proved the power of self delusion.

I don't hurt people, I don't say mean things or steal or do drugs. None of that stuff. I'm sure everyone lies, I'm sure everyone is so insecure they have to sleep with their ex-boyfriends even though he's in a new relationship.

This lie had become almost a prayer, I recited it so often. Yeah, I didn't go around shooting people and I didn't shop lift or start bar fights, but that sure as hell didn't make me a good person. Good people didn't sleep with men in relationships, didn't lie to said man in hopes of ruining said relationship. I was in my bedroom, I'd taken off work a little early to meet with him, and I was sitting in my desk chair. My hands were shaking and I felt sick.

Did I have a single friend, relative or acquaintance that I hadn't lied to? Even my closest friends didn't know the whole truth, about my failed marriage, about my family and especially not about my ex-boyfriend. No wonder I didn't really feel close to anyone, no wonder I felt alone. I had built myself a prison, one lie, one selfish decision, one rationalized moral divergence, at a time. My whole life was a sham. I had lied so often and so effectively I had almost, almost convinced myself of them.

I wondered if this was what dying was like in the sense that my entire life seemed to flash before my eyes. I tried to discover when my path had veered off into the darkness. Had I always been a liar or was it something I'd developed along the way? Did it really matter?

All of this was headed by the knowledge that if I were to come 'clean', fess up to all my friends, I probably wouldn't have any left. But, I reasoned, considering none of them truly knew me, had they ever really been my friends? I hadn't given them the chance to find out. I began to see how someone could lose their entire lives in being someone they weren't, dredged down in fear and desperation. I realized that I had shackled myself so neatly and so securely that there was no way out. Eventually my castle was going to come crumbling down around me. I knew enough, I could admit enough, to know that the truth, inevitably, always comes out in the end.

Would I continue on as I had been, layering and fortifying my little lair until I slipped up, until someone was perceptive enough to look just a little bit closer? Or would I choose the moment of my unmaking, would I rally what little dignity and morality I had left and be honest, starting with myself.

"I'm a bad person," I said aloud, tasting the words, getting a feel for their weight. I felt simultaneously cold inside yet somehow lighter. "I am a liar," I said. I was shaking now; my body warring between crying and vomiting. Maybe both. "I have hurt others." It felt surreal, my mind automatically trying to object.

I don't hurt people, I don't say mean things or steal or do drugs. None of that stuff. I'm sure everyone lies, I'm sure everyone is so insecure they have to sleep with their ex-boyfriend.

I squashed this mind set. I shredded the words mentally. I was crying, which felt wrong somehow. My misery was of my own creation, did I have any right to cry about it?

"I don't want to be this person anymore," I said.

It was the first step on a very long, and lonely road. But whenever I got low, so low it didn't seem worth it anymore, I'd remember that moment, and it reminded me of what low was. Low is losing all faith in yourself, is realizing who you are under the layers of your own pretentious bullshit. Low is living a life that isn't your own. ❖

Burning Of The Barren Tree

J.C. Baez

Illustrates the First Sin of Man and the process of overcoming this and other traumatic experiences, by leaving it behind and picking up the peices of our lives.

First Rite Of Passage: Coming Of Age In The West

Kara Hamilton

Moving west for college with the purpose of finding some adventure and self-discovery, this collection is a self-inflicted first rite of passage from an adolescent into a young adult. Craving change and growing tired of the sleepy Midwest skies and wanting to start over in a land that was completely strange and new. A first full taste of the 'Wild West,' a first splash into a desert oasis, a first night falling asleep under the stars, and a first summer as a river guide. The sense of raw exploration felt during this time will stick forever.

CAMPGROUND LIVING - Lived out here a few weeks in the summer (yes it was the summertime in this photo).

WHEN THE MOOSE SWAM - Kayaking at sunset, stumbled upon a bull moose awkwardly swimming across the lake. It was the first time seeing an animal that large and close.

MONSOON - The weather out there was raw and powerful; it wanted the adventure just as much.

SWIM - I became enchanted by water out there. I felt happy and free when finding a place to float.

YELLOWSTONE - Out there I just felt like another animal. There were so many larger animals ruling that land.

WHEN THE STORM BROKE - After a grueling day kayaking through hail and sleet, we made it to our destination. At sunset the clouds parted, and for the first time on the trip, we saw where we were.

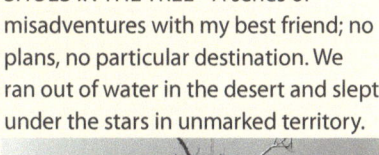

SHOES IN THE TREE - A series of misadventures with my best friend; no plans, no particular destination. We ran out of water in the desert and slept under the stars in unmarked territory.

GLACIER - For the first time I felt tiny in the eyes of nature; it crushed my ego and restored my heart.

HAVASUPAI - An oasis of waterfalls where I first fell in love with the West. The catalyst for the rite of passage.

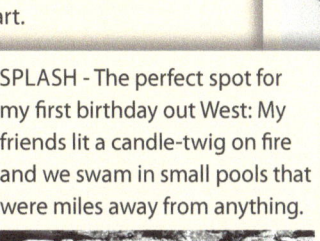

SPLASH - The perfect spot for my first birthday out West: My friends lit a candle-twig on fire and we swam in small pools that were miles away from anything.

RAPPEL - My first rappel down a canyon. We stayed too late and had to climb up the canyon walls in the dark.

EMPIRE BUILDER - I had romanticized for so long about the idea of seeing the country by train.

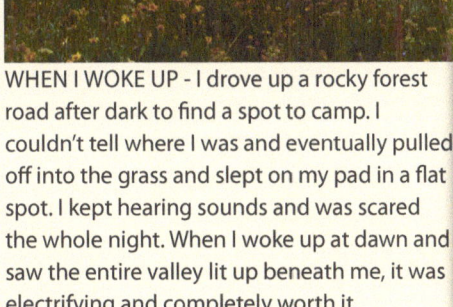

WHEN I WOKE UP - I drove up a rocky forest road after dark to find a spot to camp. I couldn't tell where I was and eventually pulled off into the grass and slept on my pad in a flat spot. I kept hearing sounds and was scared the whole night. When I woke up at dawn and saw the entire valley lit up beneath me, it was electrifying and completely worth it.

US 89 N - I really loved traveling on the road alone. The pure freedom felt knowing I could stop and go wherever I wanted was exhilarating.

Healing

Restoration where needed.

The Dahlia Garden

Ann Kendall ●●

"The Amen of nature is always a flower." - Oliver Wendell Holmes

As I've walked through the gardens of my life, I usually come back to the same ones – well-loved flowers, paths and benches for which I need no driving directions. The familiarity gives me comfort and at the same time, because the stones there no longer challenge my feet, my mind finds it easier to study treasured elements nearest to me. My walk to find faith is mirrored in those gardens – for it is there that I most likely wonder if I shall ever find a home, a place for my heart to rest when it is most weary or filled with the greatest joys. I cannot look skyward and I cannot delve inside under a constructed roof; my mind is clear that given the damp climate in which I live, each moment that it is possible to be outside is a moment to relish. The search cannot be spent inside, looking at a cross or gazing out through crisp hues of stained glass is merely a waste of time. It is only outside, in the midst of the green, gray, mist and sun that glimmers of a life beyond that the earthly mind may exist.

My roots are weak – I've spent most of my life as a maple seed twirling and picking up the next breeze fueled by fires real and imagined. These fires send me on my way, ideas may germinate but the tendrils don't grow into the earth – I've been immune. In my seed state I've traveled and when I seek solace from the journey, the dahlia garden is the place where I most often come to rest, draw and see. There are no symbols, no urgent messages – just petals, twisting and turning toward the sun. It is inside of the flowers I seek, to analyze and document with my lens the shape and color that broadcast to the world, look here and see what you can see. By looking inside each flower's whorled or conical shape, I can see the knowledge that I seek. Each color

melds to another, hues to the light from tint to shade each petal rests amongst its peers – not alone, but together, nestled – not competing. Each strong stalk grows tall though it will never reach the sky; it merely exists to hold its bulbous head high and open. While the petals grow and stretch at different rates, each seeks the rays of the sun while the stalk carries nutrition to its burgeoning leaves.

In this garden, a mirror of community grows in glorious colors from deep violet to the softest pink meld together in delicate spider-like shapes, as if they are neighbors seeking the same sustenance. The marine air of summer leaves droplets some mornings that fade as the sun makes its later afternoon debut. The dahlia is a mirror of faith that awakens slowly and while there are clear paths between the rows of stalks, each flower itself proves different, glowing and worthy. My faith– like the dahlia is sometimes speckled and fresh with a ripe new discovery after the dew yet sometimes faded and browned like the flower that is nearly done in. The dahlias understand their season and their caretakers lovingly groom the ground for their time on the earth.

My time in the garden is often in bits and broken pieces, minutes here or there, nothing really takes hold in such fits of time. Ideas remain glimmers that cannot be completed. When I develop the photos I've taken I can look at each as though I am looking at a thought from my visit; sometimes clarity and sometimes not. Each magical petal tells a story; none bears a cross – clarity comes from the beauty of the petals as they naturally merge and sway, not from conditioned response. The dahlia in its earthly know-how provides the context to hypothesize

> After pondering for several years what it means to be faithful, this particular visit was the first time acknowledging that it was both appropriate and divine to find faith while in a garden; a building was not needed.

on belief – where is it that this flower shall lead me? If it is true that I cannot find meaning inside the walls, perhaps the meaning lays clearly here within the labyrinth of petals?

It seems natural that no matter what the road taken, faith in the flowers is pure and complete. What greater act of faith could there be than to see the dahlia, from sprout to sturdy stalk to bursting flame of color – it gives forth the gift of birth and beauty, and then renewal when it is time for the petals to drop. Next year, it will return, stronger. This lesson of the dahlias I have the most difficult time in learning; I want to know the lesson, I crave to understand – how can I be more like the dahlia? How can I grow and find the path that I seek? The dahlias have taught me that there is no right path, varietals encourage an introspective speculation – but I always want to know the result, where will the road take me – even though the dahlias are clear that beauty is the fleeting moment to be enjoyed.

My walk to find faith is never clearer than when sitting with the dahlias; when I am away from them I try and try to understand the choices around me but I feel nothing but a painful ambiguity where I deem most of what I see in the world of faith as mimicry at best and farce when I am most keenly frustrated. The gates that bind through the requirements of mainline faith, do not block the entrances to the dahlia garden – there the soft grass and cedar trees call out an open invitation to come, sit, and watch – to be with the earth as it shows its possibilities to all that would consider them just as they are – magnificent and glorious. While my walk passes through the celestial garden just once, my place

with the dahlias I can visit without end. My visits to the sanctuary as deemed by others will be infrequent; but to the garden I will come often – it is only here in nature that a true amen will come forth for me, for it is here that I am grateful, humbled and in awe of my surroundings – it takes no admonition, no direction – it is complete with an unbounded joy that cannot be replicated anywhere else. The colors, the light, the flip of the wind as it catches my hair are all beauty; free and exposed – a place where faith blossoms and does not hide or cower. A faith that is awash with the spectrum of color and light that in its earnest intent, abides the heart to open.

When Holmes spoke to the Amen of nature, I ponder to which version of Amen he considered – whether he thought mostly as an end to a prayer answered, an assurance of hope or more of the notion that nature has the final word. Did the flower represent the final word then, as a culmination of a faithful undertaking whose result is petals open to the sun and sky? Unlike my maple seed self, the dahlia's symbiotic nature starting with its tuberous form, sinks deeply into the ground to grow its thick stalk and dense blooms. For the dahlia, the Amen of each flushing blossom represents not merely the finale of the growth cycle, but also the assurance that the next season will come. As the dahlia matures, each cycle represents a prayer answered, perhaps not a spoken prayer, but one of grace, toil and dedication. No dahlia grows alone, no stalk produces just one flower – it is their togetherness and reliance on nature and human that produces splendor. The dahlia's gift then is splendor split open by wonder.

(Next Page) ➔

A maple seed has a generally short life. Each seed, no matter the adventure, must eventually come to rest. It is the lucky seed that is allowed to choose its spot on the earth; most never take root, disintegrating before they have the chance and all that flitting about tends to be wearing. The luckiest of maple seeds will land near the dahlia garden, perhaps on a soft pillow of untended grass where it may take root and feel the soft sprinkle of dew each day. The dahlias may cast shadows over the maple seed to protect it from a wind; all together the dahlia garden is a formidable foe – it will protect the weakest among its own ranks, and the hapless visitor who stumbles in for a rest.

I first came to the dahlia garden as a high school girl; in my mind I see myself in a plaid skirt standing near the statue in the center of the garden with my giggling friends. There to study our horticulture text, we really knew nothing of gardens – we did not understand the difference between annual and perennial beyond book definitions. Then we were simply on the cusp of the garden's beauty and strength, we did not see how it might extend our lifetime joys or buoy us in times of sadness. The dahlias, in their perennial act of faith, stood then as they do now – open and reverent. They bloom regardless of audience, seeking no applause -- reveling in the simple act of opening. My footfalls may stumble and grow weak, perhaps veer back to the spiral of the maple seed, but the dahlia is forever in my heart. Amen. ❖

Living Sun

Kat Lahr

First time learning
to be alone
with myself,
my thoughts,
my dreams,
my demons.

First Christmas As A Single Parent

Maureen Sebek

That year was a memorable one in our lives as a family and not for reasons I was proud of. As a newly divorced single mother, only two months into the realities of single parenting, I had zero dollars to spend on Christmas and four kids who had been accustomed to very generous Christmases up until that year.

I was depressed. Not only was I grieving the loss of my marriage, but the thought of Christmas was sending me over the edge. I didn't want my kids to be on the receiving end of any further losses. The break up of our family had forced me to sell our home, move the kids into a tiny apartment, get rid of our family pet, since the apartment wouldn't allow dogs, and forced me to take a job that took me out of the home and left the kids as "latch key" kids for the first time in their lives. Now, Christmas was chasing me down and I was dreading telling my four children they shouldn't expect gifts this Christmas. I was broker than broke and feeling pretty miserable about it all. I was wishing, if there were any way possible, could we just skip Christmas that year?

But, sometimes, our kids surprise us in the most amazing ways. And that was the case that year. I sat them all down and laid the cards on the table. We didn't have any money for Christmas. Period. Just that simple. Sorry, but, that was the reality. No way to fix it. Or so I thought.

In the middle of my explanation of why we would have to cancel Christmas, my youngest son, then only ten years old, smiled at me with a grin that spread across his face from ear to ear and said he didn't see why we couldn't still exchange gifts. He suggested that we pull names from a hat and buy a gift for the person whose name we had pulled, limiting the gift to no more than five dollars. I wasn't too big on the idea but the enthusiasm he had for the plan was contagious. All the kids jumped on the band wagon and playfully embraced Matt's plan, all pretending it would be the best Christmas they had ever experienced.

They sat and mulled it over for quite a while, as if it were a master plan requiring hours of thoughtful, strategic planning. I marveled at these kids – so willing to accept, with grace and love for each other, the hand that had been dealt to them that year – the worst they had ever experienced in their young lives.

I could not have imagined the care that these kids put into their shopping that year. On the smallest of budgets, they shopped for just the right gift for each other, chosen to tickle the heart of the one on the receiving end of the gift. The entire month before Christmas was a ritual of playful teasing and guessing who had who and what had they purchased. I'm not sure they ever had more fun with Christmas.

> A young mother experiencing her first Christmas alone with her four children.

I could not tell you today what any one of those gifts was that night. As their mom, I sat and watched the love of these kids so beautifully on display as they wished each other a Merry Christmas, ending a year of heartache and pain that none of us would ever forget. The little five dollar gifts we gave each other that year were just cover! Wrapped over and under and in between those silly little gifts was the priceless message "I love you – no matter what..."

As I watched my kids celebrate Christmas that year, I realized God had used my children to teach me the meaning of real love. It cannot be broken - not by divorce, not by hardship, not by the experience of "poverty" that we found ourselves in that Christmas. Love never fails! Christmas was simply never sweeter...

1 Corinthians 13: 4-8 NKJV

"Love suffers long and is kind;
love does not envy;
love does not parade itself,
is not puffed up;
does not behave rudely,
does not seek its own,
is not provoked,
thinks no evil;
does not rejoice in iniquity,
but rejoices in the truth;
bears all things,
believes all things,
hopes all things,
endures all things.
Love never fails..."

Mindfulness

Our awareness to reality.

Blue Balled, Waiting For A Bus

Robert Tolzien

> First true heart break, where emotions are pushed far a first time, being overwhelming and disastrous.

'You're just not the friend I need you to be'
she proclaims after years of devotion I was sure would finally pay off
A friend
A best friend
A best friend I have felt drawn to since the moment I met her.
Years before, 'friends' cut it for about a month in my eyes

From there a physical attraction grew.
Noticing how her body flowed in traditional curves
Her hair as smooth and dark as a moonless sky
Her deep eyes that make me transparent
The heat between our bodies in a 'friendly' embrace
Getting caught admiring her form and getting a smirk as a response

An emotional connection thrived
Finishing each other's thoughts and sentences
Knowing with a simple look that she had had a bad day
Knowing that only the other knew exactly how to turn that day around
Knowing when an adventure out was needed or a night in splitting a bomber of craft beer
I was there through the wide array of the emotional spectrum
From the night she cried on my shoulder about being the only virgin she knew
I was there to listen about how she lost that virginity to someone who wasn't me
I was there as a shoulder to cry on when her boy toy left her
The rough times with work and family
The day her mother asked me why I wasn't dating her daughter yet
The rough times between her and I
More frequent then not

I wanted more, she didn't
Why wait 8 years to entirely split?
Our relationship ran on a cycle
6 months of inseparability

6 months of ignored calls and texts
Repetition, every time I'd ask to be with her
Without a reason why even when asked

Why in my brain I couldn't process that nothing will ever come of this is beyond me
I read all the signals and processes them as any man should
She couldn't not be in physical contact
A bit lip with a caught glance
She was the one girl I could put myself out there for only to have my heart ripped out, several times
One last final shot, ask her to be with me, and I get hit with it
The friend break up 'You're just not the friend I need you to be.'
And there I stand, blue balled, waiting for a bus. ❖

Devil When Around Me

The first crush that consumes you.

Jordan Brooks

Perspective

Theory and analysis upon desired subjects.

Original Love

Stephen Thom

I have constantly fluctuating thoughts when it comes to 'love'. Sometimes I think it is as much a cultural concept as anything else we are drip-fed through different media outlets, presented eventually in some kind of twisted form of romanticism that is of no use to anyone.

In Aristophane's speech in Plato's Symposium, he puts forward a mythical story in which, at the dawn of time, human beings were originally divided into three genders - male/male, female/female and male/female. Or male, female and androgynous. Humans were large, circular entities with two sets of everything - four arms, four legs, two heads, two sets of genitalia and so on. When we moved quickly we would roll around, cartwheeling about with our multiple limbs. However, we were overcome with our own pride and lust for power, saw ourselves as superbeings, constantly craving more. This megalomania culminated in our climbing to the heavens to fight with the gods. Zeus, in his anger, decided to exact punishment by cutting us down to size - quite literally, cutting every human being in half. Since then we have roamed the earth as incomplete parts of a broken whole, searching for our original other halves.

A short time ago I met up with a person I had previously been romantically involved with for the first time in five years. It's not an experience I've had before, so I'm aware I am probably quite naïve and uninformed in the natural emotions that might accompany such an event. The relationship had ended abruptly in less than agreeable circumstances, but it felt tremendously cathartic to sit and catch up for several hours in the same way it used to be. I think I sat in a kind of chronic miserable hump for a couple of days afterwards. I hate to relate my 'heart' to these things but I'm certain I felt such a heavy sadness in my heart during that aftermath, like I could feel it radiating in a unique way that I wasn't used to. This relatively brief conversation had fostered some kind of new chemical reaction or frequency inside me that was manifesting itself as tiny, stabbing pulses needling throughout my bloodstream.

> The first love
> that comes at our
> soul's creation.

And as much as I persevere to live relentlessly in the real world, I found myself thinking back to Aristophane's speech and contemplating in my rose-tinted, nostalgic state the possibility that she was my original other half. That part of me that I had been cut apart from, and that I was doomed to roam around eternally searching for. And I'd made a titanic mess of it. Or maybe that was the challenge that was the point? We'd had our first period of time, and certain things had come to pass, and we weren't together in that sense anymore. But I'd had the chance to see her again five years later. I was so extraordinarily glad to have been given that time, even if it was just a matter of hours. And if that little flickering link was there, that innate bond, that tiny severed line that had originally bound us together, however minuscule it may be now and regardless of what words you might attach to our current status as two people, then really this time is so precious that I should store it away. It should be another vital, intricate part of my consciousness, my spark of awareness, my fundamental make-up. And there is a tremendous hope there too - so what if it is another five years before we meet again, or ten, or twenty? Right at that exact point I could have survived the rest of my life on the nourishment of those few hours, the immense privilege of that little dose of my original love, that's fine, just leave it to course continually through my bloodstream and reverberate around my soul. I wouldn't be alone anyway (in a broad sense), because that's the biggest illusion. We're all breathing the same air, we're all made of the same elements...and my little link, my missing half could be roaming apart from me over untold distance, through centuries and millennia, and I could handle that, because I've been given this incredible time.

Or not. It's all a spectrum of possibilities, and I guess that's one thing I could have thought out of a multitude. ❖

First Love

Leemour Pelli

> First loves have multiple and dualistic meanings and impacts.

Love-space and a space of love, memory (and hence time), and perhaps pain and longing.

The impact of having a first love, or perhaps not finding that first love. Its impact of (having it or not) on one's life, soul and being.

It is one's "First Love," or about the love that one cannot actually find or attain. . . just imagined or really there?

A soul-mate type of love, or of a love no longer existing in the present, that can be haunting.

A first love unites and becomes an interior element, as opposed to the (normal) exterior that one sees. Their interiors are thus rendered visible and the viewer is given exposure to something that is not normally seen.

Its the proclivity for a poetic state or space, marked by an imprint, a condition, or fate. Perhaps a human weakness, handicap or a power, an incompleteness or fullness. Subject to over-emotional, out of control, things in hiding or tragedy and passion.

A first love is a summit of sorts, one that takes over and impacts the rest of the space or central figure(s). One questions the security and stability of this as balanced at the height of things, or out of control. ❖

Firsts: Ideas That STEM From Social Roots

Matt Haydu

Part 1: Background

When I was first asked by Kat Lahr of *Thought Collection* to produce a literary piece for their "Firsts" series, I was taken aback by the opportunity. I'm a self-taught creative writer with an educational background in business and a recreational background in the study of various scientific wonders. At the age of twenty, I fused my love for both areas and created my clothing brand, Venus Fallen. Born from several life-changing epiphanies and the business know-how to handle logistics, my company was born. To make a long story short, I am now twenty-three years young and have enjoyed every bit of existence since my "great awakening" three years ago. During this short era, I have asked myself countless amounts of questions regarding the "how" and "why" my brain suddenly adapted a new operating system tailored towards enhanced scientific literacy. What triggered the desire to shape shift the mission statement of my cerebral underpinnings? What forces were at work rewiring my biology to handle such complex, yet humbling thoughts? I came to one conclusion… my exposure to a new source of information.

Part 2: Purpose

The purpose of my "Firsts" piece is dedicated towards a new breed of mental transcendence being birthed from improved Internet technology and social capabilities. "Firsts: Ideas that STEM from Social Roots" discusses the art of abstract thinking, ultimately promoting positivity and a newfound appreciation for digital evolution. Though I believe a topic such as this could be used to create a book, which would be wonderful, this is meant to be a simple dose of rapturous wonder that will jumpstart your day with a new perspective on life.

Part 3: The Social Internet

What is arguably the greatest gift that the Internet has given us since its inception? Social networks. On a simplistic level, social networks are just online interfaces that allow for improved communication inside of a digital realm. On an abstract level, social networks contain hundreds of millions to billions of individual nodes. Each individual node is a human brain with its own ideas, outlooks, skills, etc. Think of your normal stroll down a city street and try to imagine the invisible, highly integrated system that exists simply because the Internet is accessible from a device, especially mobile. In a way, humans have developed an intricate technological web, which we enjoy being stuck in because of one major difference from a traditional [spider] web. We have the freedom to operate. Now, how does this affect enhanced social abilities for all of mankind? Here is where it gets interesting. The Internet is a playground for our virtual self representations. Each avatar carries with them our ideas and opinions on every pressing topic to ever surface in our society. Anyone who is part of a social network has instantaneous access to the ideas of those billions of other nodes mentioned before. To put it simply, we have spawned the birth of a virtual breeding ground of idea creation. Our mobile devices live their lives as digitally outsourced brains connected to our cognitive thought processes. Though they are not physically connected to us, these devices contain our personalities, our likes, our dislikes, and eventually

The first for
a generation.

become a component used to build our technological exoskeleton. As Moore's law continues to progress, humanity will begin to see an enhanced coexistence between man and machine. The Internet certainly will be regarded as the foundation for how humans began fusing their biological thoughts with mechanical entities. In this perspective, we have already become cybernetic organisms.

Part 4: Perspective & Potential

In regards to the power of information sharing and accessibility, we must also think about the historical implications from a past perspective. In the 19th and 20th century, Nikola Tesla reigned as one of the smartest men to have ever lived, yet his ability to share ideas with the global scientific community with a simple e-mail or Internet post wasn't possible. Instead, his genius suffered limitations at the cost of being born before the generation who invented social networking capabilities. My point is, idea sharing via social networks supports the exponential growth of innovation. What could Tesla have accomplished if he was apart of such a sophisticated network? I guess we can only imagine the vast possibilities. When minds are always connected wirelessly to a world of information, better ideas and faster progress is inevitable. For example, 1.) Corporations can use data mining techniques to scan the web for CRM (Customer Relationship Management) demographic information, furthering their ability to tailor specific needs to target markets. 2.) Entrepreneurs can blend the ideas from hundreds to thousands of creative minds in an effort to invent a new form of discontinuous innovation.

This is the type of innovation that births entire industries and stabilizes economies. 3.) Thinkers can build online communities promoting education, philosophy, science, and many other helpful applications to trigger healthy brain activity. If that sounds familiar, good, because you're currently experiencing that world of Internet-learning just by frequenting this wonderful website.

Part 5: The First

We are truly the first generation to experience a constant connection to an almost infinite library of facts, ideas, thoughts, and dreams. That connection continues to grow stronger. The ideas continue to reproduce. The facts progress us towards a positive future of information-rich Internet users. The one key thing for any individual experiencing this evolution is to remember the importance of finding a balance. It's great to be information-rich, but knowing how to absorb the correct information will help us transform it into usable knowledge. This usable knowledge, which is in our reach now more than ever, is the very foundation of this short literary thought experiment. If you're reading this, smile. You're one of the lucky ones. You live in a physical world that coexists parallel to a digital web of endless information. You live on an organic spaceship fueled by gravity. You're floating through the cosmos belonging to a network of self-aware brains allowing the Universe to study itself. You live your life as a unique pattern of atoms and molecules bound to every grand vision you choose to endorse and every problem you're faced with to solve. If you're reading this, just think. ❖

First Time Sin, Shame And Meat

Juliane von Kunhardt

When did mankind first start eating meat? Were we meant to eat meat and if so, in what manner? Looking to the beginning of everything takes us in the Bible to when Adam and Eve were kicked out of paradise. It was the first time ever that blood was spelt. We know the story: The apple tree ban, the snake and the sin. Suddenly Adam and Eve realized they were naked. The first time shame entered humanity. So clothes were made and in order to have leather and fur, an animal had to be killed. Genesis tells us this was the end of paradise for God's first people and animals. The first time for shame, death and - well, meat!

Echoes Of The Fall

J.C. Baez

First fall of humanity and how the effects of sin have reverberated and continue to throughout history and individually, and how the actions of the past can affect the future.

Adventures

**Annals of events chronicled
for future reflection.**

Diary Of A Wisdom Tooth Extraction

Ben Hardy at dentistry.co.uk

21 March 2010

Today is officially the first day of spring, and this year spring has been a long time coming. But the sun shone today, and I dug out a strip of lawn for our new potato bed. The reason for writing this is that tomorrow, Monday, I shall be having a bottom wisdom tooth out under general anaesthetic. I have never been put to sleep before, so only know second-hand what to expect.

I am really rather scared about the whole thing. One hears of horror stories about people dying, or worse, becoming seriously debilitated because of mishaps during minor surgery. And, of course, I am a little worried about that, to the extent that I have slept badly the last couple of nights. But I am also dreading the pain in my jaw when I wake, and even the whole process of being knocked out. My father says it is unlike being asleep; you become nothing and have no concept of self or time. And the unknown is frightening.

There are mundane procedural points to note. I have had my last supper – a rather good beef chilli, guacamole and tomato salad, with a glass and a half of wine – and I am not allowed anything but water now until after the operation. Claire will be coming with me, and taking me home. Following surgery, I must be accompanied for 24 hours, though I am not entirely clear why. The information sent out recommends that once home I wear old pyjamas for a while, which suggests I am expected to bleed copiously. I am not good with blood, particularly my own. On the plus side, Claire has filled the freezer with ice cream and the fridge with 'Thick and Creamy' yoghurt. We shall see what tomorrow brings.

22 March 2010

What a strange, and not entirely unpleasant, experience. The very worst moments were all at the beginning, and not what I was expecting to write about. Firstly, parking was awful. We left the house this morning at quarter past nine, which I thought was cautiously early for a ten o'clock appointment. I had not factored in the car park for hospital visitors being entirely full, or the 'on street' parking being limited to two hours and no return. Eventually, we left the car in a 'residents only' area about a seven minute walk from the hospital, hoping that the traffic wardens would fail to swoop. And we arrived at the dental hospital in a thoroughly bad mood.

Things did not improve once were ushered into the 'One Day Patients' waiting room. The television in the corner was vomiting out The Jeremy Kyle Show at double volume. This is one of those ghastly modern-day bear-baiting programmes where Chavs in Crisis present their personal problems to a studio audience, Jeremy Kyle (whoever he is) and anyone who cares to watch from home. The featured scenario was a live paternity test where at least two, and possibly three, young men were arguing with the 19-year-old mother. It involved

> ## First time sedated into unconsciousness and as a hospital patient.

shouting, chants and tears, and was impossible to ignore. Though I did not know it at the time, this was the absolute nadir of the morning.

Once called, Claire and I went through the ward into a consultation room. Margaret, a lovely, mumsy nurse, asked several questions, mostly verifying my identity, the operation and when I had last eaten and drunk. I think I was asked these questions four times over during the morning, once by each one of the people involved. The amount of cross-checking was comforting: it reduced the chances of having dentures fitted by mistake. Margaret offered a cream anaesthetic for my hand, where the tubes would go in, and I gratefully accepted on the basis that 'stoical' is not one of my preferred attributes. She also allowed me to keep my wedding ring on, provided it was taped over, and again I was grateful.

Next, after a short period back in the waiting room, I met the surgeon; a pretty and somewhat-too-young Asian woman whose name I have forgotten. She explained the procedure, warned me of side effects and risks, one of which was a potential permanent loss of sensation, and had me sign a consent form. Later, I was asked twice whether the signature on the form was my own. I was struck by how careful everyone was not to get the procedural elements wrong. From the surgeon, Claire and I were ushered back into the waiting room where we were now the only people and we chatted as happily as possible under the circumstances. About 10 minutes later, the door opened and I was called back to get into the hospital gown. This was it – no opportunity to escape.

Before getting into the gown, a fetching one-piece number with 'Leeds NHS Trust' written all over it in pink, yellow and brown, I met the anaesthetist, who I took to immediately. She was called Helen, had a friendly manner and face, and was probably about my age. She also explained the procedure and risks, but left me feeling reassured about the whole process. I got into my gown, got onto the bed, Margaret covered me with a silver blanket and a woollen one, Claire left, and I was wheeled into the anaesthetist's room.

Margaret put a blood pressure band round my arm and some device to measure my pulse, and the tube for administering the anaesthetic was put in the back of my right hand. I hardly felt it enter. Helen then pumped something in, claiming this was the 'fun part' and it would feel like a gin and tonic. I started to feel a little dizzy after a few seconds and she then put in the substance to send me to sleep. I felt my arm go slightly cold and stiff, I had a brief moment of wooziness, and the next thing I knew I was telling Margaret that I had been dreaming of Barbarians. So, it was not quite true that I had no concept of time passing, but the only moments that felt like proper sleep were at the very end, just as I was waking up.
In that period I had obviously been aware enough to dream of ravaging hordes, but before that, nothing.
And when I woke I could tell something had been done to my mouth, but I was not in pain. Mostly, I felt really rather drunk.

(Next Page) ➜

Time was also deceptive in the hour after the operation. Claire came to sit beside the bed and I yattered to her about what had just happened. But what felt like five minutes was nearer thirty, and apparently I had a couple of ideas which I told Claire several times over. Four hours on from this, I have little memory of that.

Margaret brought me a blackcurrant drink and went through some 'post operation' information, Claire went to get the car, I got dressed, was walked around the ward slowly and was discharged. In the car – Claire drove – I felt worse than I had in the hospital, but nowhere near as bad as I had imagined I would. And a couple of thick and creamy yoghurts and a small bowl of tomato soup helped sort that out. Probably my blood sugar levels were just low.

The local anaesthetic they gave me has gradually worn off, and I have taken a couple of painkillers, but at the moment my jaw just aches a little. I have not dared to run my tongue against the hole. Nor do I have any plans to do this soon. ❖

Traffic School

Lottie Krol ████████████████████████████ ● ●

> **Disclosure of a first time offense.**

It finally came in the mail, and when it did, big letters read "TRAFFIC SCHOOL" on the front. Really? Was that necessary? Right there for anyone to read or see, broadcasting my delinquency. It's been over 6 weeks of waiting and I almost thought they had forgotten about me. This was my first experience with something like this and I wasn't quite sure what the procedure called for. All I know is that I have always had a fear of being tasered. Let me explain…

I have a van where the driver's side window is stuck and won't roll down. Can't wait to get that fixed. This scene plays in my mind often:

I'm being stopped by an officer and he asks me to roll down my window and I, of course, can't. So I try to open the door to let him know that, but he thinks I'm threatening him, so he pulls out his taser and POOF! You get the point.

Yes, can you tell I have an active imagination? So when I didn't receive my traffic school schedule, I imagined a police officer running my plates and well, you know the rest.

Yes, it's my first experience being a delinquent. Opening the envelope, I'm secretly praying that wherever they send me, it has good parking and isn't too far away. To my surprise, they gave me an online course. Praise God! He is aware of all my inadequacies and decided to show mercy upon me. Now, all I have to do is learn how to sign in and use the program correctly! ❖

Rain, And More Rain

Kat Lahr

> **First time having respect for the power and control the weather can have.**

Its 3:00 am and something woke me up. It's been raining for about 12 hours straight now and I have been sleeping like a baby up to this point. The sound of the rain on my windows always hypnotized me and it was still going. For a few seconds I relished in the rhythm of its music. No thunder, no lightening, just rain and more rain. I noticed my husband wasn't next to me and I heard bustling of some sort downstairs. I immediately felt like something was wrong as if the energy of my husband's franticness found me in our bedroom. I no longer heard the music. I swiftly rose from the bed to get a grip of what was going on.

"We have water" he said as he quickly shuffled nervously down the basement stairs. As quickly as I heard the splash of the water from his boot hitting the water at the bottom, I felt a rush of anxiety. I followed halfway then crouched and watched him through the bars of the wood railing, like a child peeking in curiosity as he examined our sump pump. I could feel the frustration that was erupting from the lack of control he had. The sound of the water moving around his feet was not the same music of the rain water on the window. It was loud, disturbing and screeching to my ears.

I didn't say a word for what felt like eternity, as my eyes looked around at the ruins of what we worked so hard to have. I lived in apartments almost my whole life and just bought the house a year and a half ago. We decorated our basement to remind us of our honeymoon in Hawaii. The soft blue and light brown walls resembling the beaches held the pictures of hula, the dried petals of our leis and the colors of hibiscus flowers. The space held our first Christmas as a married couple, our daughter's first ice cream social with her friends, our first wine tasting and hours of Guitar Hero and Monopoly. Floating and sinking in over a foot of rain and sewer water were the pieces of our life together:

- Empty wine bottles from our winemaking hobby.
- All the children's books I have been keeping since my daughter was little for our unborn son I was currently expecting.
- The telescope we saw the rings of Saturn and the moons of Jupiter through as we fell in love on the balcony of our first apartment together.
- The futon, our first piece of furniture we bought together.
- Our new kitchen cabinets we so proudly hand stained and installed ourselves over the summer.
- All slowly being ruined as water filled the crevices of everything it touched.

Being pregnant, there was little I could do. I watched as my husband attempted to get the water out with the small pump we use for draining our hot tub. The amount coming in was not less than the amount that small pump was getting out. I woke up my daughter to tell her what was going on and to reassure her that everything was going to be ok. It was now 4:00 am and I decided to go outside to see and smell the rain, a common exercise for me when it stormed. Out front the rain had formed a lake that came up to our front steps. Water covered everything else that use to be there; sidewalks, grass, bushes and the street. Many people had already moved their cars, some attempting to do so. Thankfully our car was in the garage, I told myself, which prompted me to check it out. The alleys were completely full with water up to everyone's garage doors. Garbage cans were floating down the street as if a current had been established by a river.

(Next Page) ➔

Between our sump pump and the hot tub pump working continuously, the water finally started to lower in our basement. However the rain kept on coming. It was relentless. At this point the radar showed about 6-8 hours of rain still to come.

Now at 5:30 am my husband finished cutting up and removing the soaked carpet as the water was almost gone. As I looked outside through our front bay window, I watched as the water crept up to our rock barrier surrounding the rose bushes at the front of our house. Inches were left before the water would spill over the rocks and begin to enter our basement windows. I was terrified. All the work to get the water out, and it was possible it could come right back in through the windows. I noticed that the bottom stairs of our front porch were now covered. I heard police sirens and wondered where they are coming from? It started to rain harder and for the first time in my life, I wished it would stop raining.

It's now 9:00 am and the rain was still falling, yet very light. Our basement continued to get water but we were able to catch it as it started. People were driving down our block very fast to try to get through the water. This created ripples and waves of water that just pushed up onto everyone's front yards and houses. I could hear my neighbor across the street yelling at all the cars that did this. Eventually the police put up barriers to keep the cars from driving through.

At 10:30 am the rain would stop then start again. We were literally stuck in our homes. We couldn't leave out the front because water came up 2 steps of our porch and the street was now a lake. The alleys were full of water and into our garage about 6 inches. Somehow the water had not yet tipped over the rock barriers to spill in through our basement windows. Channel 9 news stated we had historic rainfall, twice the normal amount of the entire month of April rain, in just 2 days.

At 11:00 am our sump pump failed after being overwhelmed all night and morning pumping out water. Within the 15 minutes, 3 inches of water filled the basement again. The hot tub pump was just not cutting

it anymore now that our sump was done for. My husband had to somehow manage to get our truck out of the garage and through the water to find a store that had a sump pump. A few hours later he called to report that he had been to 4 stores already and all were sold out of pumps. He had a few more places to try before coming back home yet the flooding all over our area made it hard for him to get around. I told him that the water was now up to 6 inches in the basement and was rising slowly but surely. He suggested I ask the neighbor if he had an extra pump of some sort to help out in the meantime.

Thankfully, he did. He had a pump he used to drain his pool, which was bigger than our hot tub pump. He came by and he set it up and 30 minutes later we still had several inches of water, but it was decreasing. The two of them together still couldn't keep up with what the sump pump did on its own, but at this point was better than just letting the water in and do nothing.

At 4:00 pm the rain had completely stopped. The radar showed it was finally over. I was obsessed with looking through the bay window and starred at it thinking for several hours about what our next steps were going to be. I thought about how ironic it was that our city, finally after many years, started its flood mitigation project earlier that week. I thought about how last summer we didn't get much rain, and were considered in a drought with irregular heat at 103-104 degrees Fahrenheit.

At 5:30 pm my husband came home with what felt like the last sump pump available to buy in our big city. A few hours later, the new pump was installed and only 2 inches of water remained. We couldn't flush the toilets, or take a shower. Finally at 9:00 pm, not only did the lake start to recede in the front, we managed to get all the water out from the basement.

At 11:00 pm we went to bed. My husband said, "If it floods again tonight, who cares, the damage is already done." We were exhausted yet tossed and turned all night. Because we were born, raised and still living in a big city, flooding, tornados and hurricanes were not the norm for us. I didn't really know how to feel. The next day my husband took the day off at work to begin gutting the basement to keep the bacteria from proliferating. No water in the basement this morning. The new sump pump did its job.

Over the next few months we renovated our basement. We were blessed to have received money from insurance to replace much of what we lost physically. I eventually became very grateful for this experience. It not only made us very intimate with the basement of our new home, it taught me to appreciate the memories we hold on to, as money couldn't replace our emotional loss. As to make the renovation affordable, we did most of the work ourselves, helping me get over my perfectionism. At first I thought I would never be able to sleep like a baby again as I listened to the music of the rain after that April, but instead, I learned to respect Mother Nature. I can still become happily hypnotized from its rhythm knowing that lessons are meant to be learned. ❖

Conceptual

Ideas conceived in the mind.

Native American Olive 1 & 2

First patterns that started to emerge from early civilisations.

Evil Eye Circle

Aboriginal Purple

EzzyPezzy

Mother Nature Gets Started

Melody Croft

What would men be like today if a feminist had created the first one? The freedom to explore life beyond the rigid boundaries of traditional masculinity and choose how he will be defined by the world.

The concept of 'Mother Nature' first appeared during the Age of Enlightenment, in response to peoples' desire to understand the physical world. Prior to, God and Nature were analogous.

The idea that nature was a separate entity from God was blasphemous. The leaders of the Enlightenment believed that in order for the physical world to be examined, nature had to be separated from God. Out of this thinking, came the belief that God (being male) had created nature, which was female. Only in this exploited form, could Mother Nature be studied. Reintroducing the pre-Enlightenment idea that nature and God are analogous, presenting the idea of the Creator as a feminine entity.

Mother Nature Puts Final Touches On Man

Melody Croft

Expression

A manifestation of a disposition.

Baby

Nithya Narayanan

> Raw anticipation of pre-motherhood. The telling of a woman waiting on her first child; the gift of life.

Five drops of blood
They escape me in a flood
They are the things I cannot do
The things I never knew

I wish he'd stay; look back
Get me back on my track
Devour me in lusty sips
Taste my ear with soft brown nips

But really, he only stares;
and met with several glares,
retreats; the lost advisor
Leaving me; the poor miser

In the morning he'll be civil
Act like I won't shrivel
Make me toast in a bed
littered with the things we never said

And we'll sit; knees apart
watching strangers make lemon tart
but really I'm looking at his untamed face
thinking about things I can't retrace

And then slowly he'll turn over- "I'm really tired"
But what, I think, about the kids you never sired?
I'll sit in darkness with a hole in my chest
A pain in my tummy; a night without rest

In the morning sun will stream
With all the things I could not dream
Thinking about my baby-
He will come someday, maybe

The first woman a boy loves is his mother.

Mums Dress

Jordan Brooks

Last Time I Saw You

Jordan Brooks

First big break up is
always the hardest.

The Night's First Necklace

That first sense of truly missing a lover long gone.

Jeri Frederickson

Tonight I wear my forgotten
lover's necklace
and slip into the black dress
I've never worn. It still fits.
My tummy is smaller
now. I twirl round my room
the door closed, exposing
the long mirror to plunging Vs
in my front and back with silky black

gathering at my knees and the smooth
stones draped over my collar bones,
the big tear stone resting atop and dipping
between my breasts. Turquoise – beauty,
good luck and magic – he said –
don't take it off.
I didn't until I returned
home. No more

mi amor, mi pequeña amor
Te amo
puedes quedar
no puedo
sí, puedes vivir conmigo
¿siempre?
Sí
Sí podría

Wear the necklace I'm giving
you, my young love, he said.
And I made love to him in it,
and I flew home in it.

And tonight I wear it again. I slip
out of the little black dress
I may never get to wear. I wear

his gift of love and blessing
for always. I am in the recesses
of his mind, getting annual, generic,
mass emails. I haunt his contact list.

Tonight I put him between my neck
and the crevice of my legs. I clutch him in
the folds of my brain. I shower with turquoise
drops beading down my thighs
and his goatee is once again

brushing my shoulder, the crook
of my elbow, the curve of my last rib
and our sweat's evaporating the Querétaro night.
I slide between my sheets alone,
rubbing the teardrop stone, my distant lover
against me one more night.

A First Date

Imani Sims

The beautiful tension we hold in our bodies when meeting someone new and enjoying the first connection.

she pulses me electric.

tiny atoms flow between
the space of our fingertip almost touch
tension, you know that moment of initial
shyness curled tightly round your abdomen,

the one that forces moths
to surface, incessant lunar light flutters
against stomach lining, pheromone signature
hits wind.

She enters me on inhale, permeated
nasal passages respond, send a message
from seven to one.

my pulse races, corners of mouth
turn to grin and I am transported
to the imagined, the place where I touch
her for the first time, all cocooned
caress and subtle break.

Every forefinger trace widens
the crack in restraint, layers fall
away, kept promises flake onto
ground, limbs begin to stretch,

laze about surrender.

Like wind, my frame wants to rest
against her, pull in. Ride the cadence
of body's guidance.

It's 4:32 am and the only tension
is image after image of what could happen.

The idea of her
pulses me electric, chases shadows
to the dark corners of bedroom,
leaves me restless, creator of the imagined.

Discovery

**Experience allows the
ability to form reactions
and learn.**

Mary, Mary, First Foster Child Of Mine

Maureen Sebek

Mary was a beautiful little girl, who came into our lives at the oh so tender age of two. Already, this little darling had been placed under the supervision of the State of Illinois and began the impossible journey of navigating the turbulent waters of the foster care system into which she had been thrust by the Department of Children and Family Services. I was a young mother of two small children, one a two year old little girl the same age as Mary, and a six month old baby boy, both of whom were the delight of my life as a young mother. My husband, a social worker and family counselor, so wanted to go beyond our four walls and minister to some of the hurting children who were in need of a good home. We had only been married three years when we took this little lost lamb into our home.

Unlike my husband, I had no concept of the myriad rules and regulations and bungled mistakes of the foster care system that so often led to tragedies in the care of these innocent victims of the system. I was about to find out first hand.

Mary came to us on a bright summer's day. In my naivete, I hoped it was a harbinger of the wonderful life Mary would have living in our home. It was far from the reality of what was coming.

Almost immediately, my daughter, the same age as this new little intruder, began to move backward in her development. Once a happy, friendly and bright child, she began to retreat into her own little world, sucking on her fingers anxiously, attempting to figure out if she was being replaced. From her little two year old eyes, it must have seemed like we were looking for a replacement for her. First we brought home a new baby that rapidly pushed her out of the center of our world. Now, adding insult to injury, we had added another child – same age, same gender as my daughter, Christy. This little interloper, deeply insecure and trying to understand her own terrifying world, was challenging Christy's little two year old world from the instant they woke up until they went to bed at night. Both children were threatened and frightened by the enormous changes that were swirling all around them.

To make matters worse, I discovered in a meeting with the Social Worker in charge of Mary's "case" that there had been no real reason to move Mary other than the whim of the Social Worker. I was shocked beyond belief. Mary had been born to severely mentally ill parents who met and conceived her at a half way house for mentally ill patients. The Social Worker informed me that, although the mother would never be able to have custody of Mary, neither would the State terminate her parental rights. Mary would be a ward of the State until she turned eighteen and "aged out of the system."

Now that was bad enough news. But the real icing on the cake was that Mary had been placed, as a newborn, in a home with two older adults who simply adored this little girl, who must have been such a blessing in their lives later in life. They doted on Mary, giving her everything they had materially and emotionally. They would never have the opportunity to adopt her, but that didn't matter to them. They loved her deeply, as if she were their own. Why then was she moved out of their home? Because the Social Worker decided the foster parents were too old and too doting on this little girl. Not because she was being neglected. Not because she was being abused. But simply because the Social Worker, with a power that reigned supreme in this little family's life, decided she didn't

In a lifetime of parenting four biological kids and 12 foster children, an initiation into the foster care world.

like the foster parents "spoiling" this little waif, who was completely dependent on a system that saw her as little more than a number that had to be accounted for until the magic age of eighteen.

I watched as Mary struggled to understand what had happened to her world. Where were the only parents she had ever known? Where had they gone? Why had they "given her away?" How could she possible have understood what had happened to her world – she was only two years old. I watched her struggle to please us, to imitate my own daughter who called us Mommy and Daddy. Where were her Mommy and Daddy? Then to add to the tremendous insecurity and confusion, the Social Worker decided it would be best for Mary to meet her "real" mother, a woman diagnosed as a severe Paranoid Schizophrenic, who seldom connected with the real world. The first (and last) time this woman came to my house for a visit was traumatizing for me, not to mention my children, including my little Mary. Mary, who had taken to calling me Mommy, sat across the table from this stranger, who informed her in a loud, combative voice, that she was her Mommy and that Mary should call her that. The confusion and fear on this little girl's face was more than I could bear. I refused to let this woman visit my home again.

By now, my husband's concerns for our own daughter had escalated to the point of no return. He called the Social Worker and asked to have Mary placed back in the original home that she had been removed from. The Social Worker, not willing to admit she had made an error in moving Mary in the first place, removed Mary from our home and placed her in yet another foster home, beginning a cycle for Mary of constant instability and new placements every six months or so, until I lost contact with where she had gone. Although the Social Worker had promised me that I would be able to keep in touch with Mary, I discovered the hard way that the system did not allow any way to track where she was and, in fairly short order, I lost contact with her forever.

At the time, I was broken emotionally over the loss of this little girl who had planted both feet in my heart and has never completely left. I grieved for her as if she was my own. Even today, as I write this story, my memories of Mary are colored with sorrow and the pain of the loss of a child I loved.

I wonder today, where are you Mary? Did you make it, Sweetheart? Are you OK? Did you know I loved you? I pray for you today that I will see you again someday. If not here, then, certainly in heaven. You deserved so much more than we were able to give you. But I know the One who holds you in His hand. I hope you have found the One Who fashioned you for a purpose, Who calls you by Name, Who died that you would belong to Him. I hope you found Jesus. ❖

First Estate Sale

Lottie Krol

A first encounter
that leads us on
necessary paths.

When I saw the notice, something leapt from the page -- couch. I have been wanting to replace my futon in the living room for a while now. Keeping my options open, I've looked at sales in stores for a brand new one and even used ones. I'm always looking for a bargain.

Never really been to an Estate Sale before, but after reading the advertisement, something urged me to go. My niece simply adores them so I asked her to join me.

Pulling up to the residence, we both admired the home's structure and outside appearance. Inside, looked like a remodel hadn't been done in the last 20-30 years. Yet as I went from room to room, I fell in love with the home. Work was badly needed, but the layout was beautiful. It just simply worked.

Walking from room to room, the house's treasures all laid out, being sold for a fraction of their worth. Eagerly, I searched for that couch because in my mind, that's why I was there. When I did finally find the couch, it was a disappointment. It needed an overhaul just like the house itself.

I walked through that house twice, revisiting each room again and again, not really knowing what I was looking for at that point. In my hands I held two porcelain bowls, total cost of $3.00. This person was selling all their possessions and all I could find were these two bowls.

Heading towards the cashier I spotted a box on a recliner that I didn't see the last two times I passed through. Opening the box, I found a treasure. It was filled with the most intricate, artistic yarn I've ever seen. The type you only find in specialty stores. Digging deeper into the box, I pulled out unfinished work so beautiful, done in patterns I haven't seen before. The artist was truly gifted and talented. I wanted this box no matter how much it was priced for.

Leaving, the cashier thanked me for coming because the owner was a senior citizen in need of money. I came in looking to buy a couch and instead I walked out with someone's talent in my hands. This yarn is meant for something special. I don't know what I will use it for, but I know there is a project lined up for me and it involves this yarn. The couch will have to wait. ❖

The artist notes that she has used the yarn to begin crocheting as an outlet to help redirect focus on something other than the Ovarian Cancer she survives from. From this discovery, she founded a Crocheting Ministry that enables individuals to use their crafting talents to benefit communities around the world by making blankets, hats and scarves for the homeless, crisis centers, women's shelters and hospitals. She is open to talking with others who may want to start a crocheting ministry in their own town.

Learn more about her ministry from our interview with her at thoughtnotebook.org/one-to-know.html

1573

Zeta Sin

A first attempt at art worth saving and sharing.

Music Of Implied Realities

Kat Lahr

Thought Collection Publishing believes in promoting all forms of art expression. As with all things that come from thinking, music has the ability to transcend us in many ways into the natural rhythm of our lives. Music is very emotional and can take us to another place with just the presence of sounds, it touches our memories and experiences. In alignment with promoting the practice of thinking, BEING, is a progressive rock band from Orlando Florida, whose sound comes from their interests in science, logic and reason. Their artistic expression is used to convey progressive thought in our lives.

When listening to their music, I could not help but think about the cosmos, the nebulaeic dust that our souls are made from. The sounds allowed me to experience the cosmic rhythm as it's heard from the ears of the suns and the galaxies. The sounds of what it's like to travel through a nebula or listen to a supernova. I felt attuned to the sounds of the sky and found myself calm from their soft catchy grooves, stimulated lyrics, and an evolved approach to metal. I felt as though I was taken to a very different conscious place where the music provided a medium for my mind to flow.

Thought Notebook got to speak with BEING's Lead Singer, Cas Haruna, about their upcoming debut album as well as tap into some of their visionary thoughts that define their band and their music.

The name of your band is BEING. What does 'BEING' mean and why did the band choose this name?

We wanted something universal and at the same time specific. The name itself is a dualism, both finite and infinite, all of which depends on the context of the viewer's perspective. A human being? Being alive? Being present? To BE? All of these interpretations play into the finite fundamental universality of 'being,' the experience of coming into existence within this Cosmos, as a piece of itself, trying to learn what it is, from within.

Your worldwide debut album, *Anthropocene* is due to come out soon. When can we expect the release?

Due to almost 2 years of constant and persistent difficulty and setback, we have yet to set a release date. It's really unfortunate, but completely outside of our control. Listeners can get clips of

the album here:
www.soundcloud.com/beingmusic.

What does this term Anthropocene mean?

We back the definition: The Era in which humankind is the primary geologic force at work shaping the present and future of this planet Earth. Call us old fashioned, or by the books, but this suits our implied meaning for the debut's title best.

It is currently being argued amongst scholars, scientists and the like, as to when the Anthropocene Era began. When do you suspect that the actual Era started?

We mark it at the dawn of the Industrial Era, where Man became the sole most powerful shaper of our Earth and its surface as we know it. The Scientific Era shortly followed in company with Industrialization, and while some consider it better marked at the advent of the Nuclear Age, or Information Age or even Internet Age.

Our human influence on the Earth is very great. What do you think is the driver behind our massive impact?

Socially: Language, and as a result, writing. Scientifically: Industrialization, but more importantly the scientific knowledge that came hand in hand that allowed us to understand reality by its most fundamental building blocks: first the periodic table, then the atom and finally the subatomic world. When we understood as a species that this reality was comprised of and composed from a finite set of building blocks, we could start to see what kind of reality we could create and impose upon, that actually we are only just now beginning to understand.

I am interested in more of your transcendentalist thoughts since you support logic, reasoning, science and thinking…

Of course, I'm ready for both your best, and your worst! Let's get in there and see what we find!

Let's start with a big one! What do you think is the ultimate fate of the universe?

This is a tough one! I am a Cosmological Physics major in college, albeit on academic leave to produce music full time. Despite that, none of us in the band, among our peers, or even in the top echelons of the high sciences themselves, know how this will all end. There are several competing theories from the Big Rip, to the Big Crunch, to even the Big Freeze. One thing everyone can agree on; the Universe has just gotten starting doing what it does, based on its finite laws of nature. We have only begun to scratch that surface of understanding as a people in our small little unremarkable corner of space. Until there is more data to support a grand ending, we in BEING like to focus on the geological timescale that we as finite biological organisms can comprehend.

There is one fact we cannot avoid: our sun has 6 billion years of fuel left, give or take a couple billion. Thereafter, it will swell up, destroy the inner solar system and burn out. Our solar system will, for a fact, inevitably die because of this. Our planet, no matter what we (realistically) do, is doomed. This leaves our species and it's biology two options: we can make our time here until the ultimate fate as good as we can, or, we can take it a step further and use our time to be not only a planetary sentient species, but furthermore an interplanetary, interstellar sentient species. It may sound like science fiction, but there is no avoiding this fact. We must find new homes around younger stars, or die with our own. These are the only two fates for our story here on Earth, and call me optimistic, but Carl Sagan has not only inspired me to subscribe to the latter, but eloquently shown how such a fate is realistic, rational, and within our grasp as we currently know ourselves intellectually on this planet. Why die in the little home town we were born in, when there's a whole universe waiting to be explored? I expect more of our human race and of our potential in this reality. We can and have done great things. To me, we have only just begun.

Do you think we are all connected? If so, what do you think is the purpose?

It all depends on context. In the sense that we all are at the whim of the laws of nature and the nearly infinite variables of those laws' interactions, I'd have to say, yes, we are. Let me elaborate a bit into what I mean. BEING supports the notion that there is in fact finite truth, as well as infinite fallacy in our world. Much of our world is caught up in the infinite fallacy of their own interpretations of what this world actually is, what their place in it could and should be, and how we all compare and contrast to the cold mechanisms of this reality. This is difficult for sentient animals like us humans here on Earth because we do not understand the differentiation of the two realities we experience every day. The first reality, is the actual reality, that is finite, follows a set of natural laws and can be known and understood through the gathering, interpreting, and testing of the data we acquire through experimentation in this world. The actual reality is reality as it actually is, in the sense of how it actually works, UNOBSERVED by any mind or sense. For example, a rock on Mars is a rock on Mars. The rock follows a specific set of laws which are naturally given through the interactions of physics, chemistry, geology, mathematics and the other high sciences. It is only when an observer is introduced, that an implied

(Next Page) ➔

reality is superimposed upon actual reality. Opposed to actual reality, which is finite, implied reality is infinite. This is because, through observation, an infinite number of interpretations upon the actual reality will spring forth and make themselves known to the experiencer. Let's go back to that rock on Mars. The moment we observe it, we imposed implied characteristics that are interpretive and thus much less solid in their reality onto the rock. We see "redness", we calibrate its weight, composition, position, and relation to a whole set of variables. We wonder what that rock's purpose is, how it got there, what it "means", not only completely, but to us individually, and as a species on Earth. These are all additional implications that if absent, absolutely do nothing to prevent that rock from continuing to be a rock on Mars, following its set laws given by nature. We do the same thing with art. It is all interpretive, so, in a lot of ways, art is almost entirely an implied reality.

What we try to do with our music at BEING is present actual reality artistically, in a way that even if the end result winds up interpreted into an infinite amount of implied realities, the actuality of its fundamental presentation remains unchanged. We are by no means perfect at doing this yet, but it's a journey, and thus far we've enjoyed the ride.

The purpose is to present art in a way that musically MEANS something. Popular culture is flooded with implied realities that are so far from what this life actually IS, that we often find ourselves left wanting when we listen to adjacent artists. Our most fundamental approach with music, is to allow for implication when our artistry is received, but hope that when all that implication is stripped away, there is an actual, factual, finite fundamentality that remains, unquestioned and undebatable. A comparison would be that despite the infinite amount of interpretations of the Mona Lisa, we all can understand and recognize the fundamentality of her smile. No one will see her to be frowning, and, we think, all who view should be able to relate to that finite, actual reality of human emotion we all share. If we can do this with our music, both through actual science and implied emotion, we consider our artistry a success. We are always on a search for the truth. We are constantly asking questions.

Why do we have this inherent need to know where we come from and ask the questions we do?

To us, this is just a misconception in what our biological need to "know" really is. First, let's take a step back to biological life prior to the inception of sentience. We had fundamental, actual necessities in order to survive.

> "...art is almost entirely an implied reality."

Beyond food, water, shelter and reproduction, there was an even more, albeit somewhat less concrete, variable driving all of life on this planet: adaptation and progression. Sure, not all branches of the evolutionary tree progressed positively, and some adaptations (most, for that matter) lead to dead ends, localized survival and eventually, extinction. This need to "know" is the natural, biological response to our consciousness. We apply it EXACTLY like non sentient life applies adaptation. We look at this world, try to understand the variables at play effecting us and wonder how we can exploit, adapt and progress beyond what we currently know; much the same as before when we'd use the very same three mechanisms to get more food, have more children, live longer lives and pass more of our genes on successfully to the following generation. A lot of the time (most, for that matter) we get this sentient step wrong, as we do so many things that are counterintuitive to our survival, adaptation and progression. Our need to know is really no surprise. It would make less sense if life had evolved to this point and just…stopped caring and didn't look to the stars, didn't question what we sensed, didn't try to build off of what we experienced and didn't see any merit in doing these things. We like to think we are beyond instinct in our modern world, but we feel that a lot of instinct SHOULD, WOULD, and in fact DOES drive us to push our mental experience just as much as our physical one in our lifespan. Personally, I feel the failure of a conscious being is becoming content and stagnant. This is because to do so prior to this consciousness of ours, would almost certainly mean the extinction of our species. This issue has not gone away; it's just a shame that we have yet to understand that we MUST care, we MUST question, and we MUST continue wanting to KNOW; and not just believe, KNOW. There is a big difference, and we spend much of our creative time illustrating how we, as artists, view and practice that difference.

Why are we emotionally driven to science and outer space?

While we are young, and many of us in school, for some of the first times in our lives, we just GET IT. It's that sensation when you FEEL, and not just feel but KNOW, without doubt, and through evidence supported by data, that what we currently comprehend, is actually, factually and finitely true. A basic example is when we all first grasp the full ramifications of 2+2=4. We understand the variables, see

(Next Page) ➜

why they represent what they do, comprehend how they interact to bring out the predicted result and finally how that result can, should, and always will be expected from the same set of variables, settings and criteria that led to the realization in the first place. No one questions the sum of 2 and 2, much like no one questions the spherical nature of our planet and much like no one questions the solar centric nature of our solar system. The latter two had to be vetted for over 2,000 years before it was finally accepted. We often get discouraged that Science has been around for 150 years and we are still in many ways living in the social Bronze Age of superstition and special interaction. While it can be a letdown in a current moment, we try to always remember that the prior 2,000 years of progress compared to the last 150, are night and day. Those who doubt science haven't given it much chance nor much time to unfurl the truths of this reality. Soon, and sooner than later, those who doubt science won't have the option. It will be comparable to doubting the sum of 2 and 2. When will this take place? We like to use the term "The Singularity" which is also the name of our two part final of our album, Anthropocene. It will be, without any doubt, the most historical, lifestyle and socially changing moment in our people's time on this Earth to date. We eagerly await this moment and hope to see it within our lifetimes.

Anthropocene is, in so many ways, our musical attempt to make aware and help to usher in this moment that couldn't come sooner. Our planet, and not just humanity, but every life form alive and yet to be born, desperately needs us to reach this point. To not do so, to us, means utter and complete failure as a sentient species and furthermore disaster and destruction of our planet's fragile state. This is what inspired the overall concept behind this debut.

What do you think is the most important awareness we can then have?

Education, and the quality therein, is without question to us the most important kind of awareness. We must go further to say that this education must consist of real learning. One can be plenty educated on Big Foot, but that knowledge is, realistically as best as we can tell from the data, moot; both plenarily speaking, and in the eyes of the universe. Science and mathematical literacy is paramount to a nation's success on so many levels and it's just as paramount to our success, progression and survival as a species. With education we must learn to inapt quality control through skepticism and scrutiny, as well as develop tools like discipline and responsibility. This will not only allow us to take what we can learn into ourselves individually, but share actual education to all we can. People have given their lives for the truth. They have been murdered to protect and to hide the truth. The truth is what gives political parties power, global nations greatness and whole cultures their identity. Learning to become educated in truth through discipline and responsibility, while being skeptical and scrutinous enough, will allow us to be able to sift through what is REAL reality and what is interpreted or implied reality. If we can do this as a species before we destroy ourselves, we have, in our opinion, truly made it.

Which came first, the chicken or the egg?

Scientifically speaking eggs existed for millions of years before the first bird-like creature, "Archaeopteryx", and were laid by dinosaurs, fish, and vertebrates and invertebrates alike. So, if the question is really, was the chicken or the CHICKEN egg first, the answer becomes simple.

The genetic mutation that led to "chickens" as we know them, first happened within the egg of the parent species. This means that, until that first chicken with the genes of "chicken ness" is hatched and thus born, no chicken egg may be laid. Therefore, we have to end this the exactly the same as we started it; much like the debut itself: it's all about context. ❖

SURVEY OF THOUGHT

We polled the thoughts of our online community.

Which Came First?

The Chicken 25%
The Egg 50%
Neither 25%

FEATURED THOUGHT OF THE WEEK

" I'm from a lot of generations, but not that one. "
-Carolyn

thoughtnotebook.org/most-recent

FEATURED COLLECTIVITY EXERCISE

Thoughts from the collective.

Dont Act Like You Don't ___ .

Gail
  think nobody is looking

Jeanne
  know why I am angry
  with you

Lottie
  care

Denise
  know

Aubrey
  understand what I'm going
  through

Tom
  get distracted easily

thoughtnotebook.org/collectivity

STAY UP TO DATE

Join our mailing list to receive our newsletters, announcements, and featured literary and visual art.

eepurl.com/CuL35

Visit our Community Website to comment about the artistry on display in this issue and how they connected with your life.

thoughtnotebook.org/thoughtistically-speaking.html#

GIVE US A THUMBS UP
facebook.com/thoughtcollection

GIVE US A RATING

Goodreads
Amazon

NEXT ISSUE

The holidays are approaching for many, which means the end of the year. Time for review and reflection for most people. Why give up something for the New Year? What about gain? What about desire? How about renewal?

Renewal means different things to different people. It can mean the need to churn something up, to remove and then transform into something else.

Consider submitting your Renewal themed literary and visual art for our next journal issue. Submissions due by March. 1st, 2014.

See all of our open and regular submission calls at
thoughtcollection.org/submissions

Reach The World With Your Work

•• Our Artists ••

Brianne McDonald

Born and raised in sunny Arizona with a few sporadic moves in-between but the desert keeps bringing her back. A full time government lackey and a dedicated single mother who spends most of her time trying to mold her daughter into enjoying all things 'nerdy' and creative. History, comic book, fantasy, computer dork who has no formal writing training and just makes it up as she goes along. Most of her works center on the fantastic but has recently dabbled in non-fiction under the idea that if you can't write well as yourself, how can you expect to write well as anyone else? Is in the process of completing the first of what she hopes will be many novels. See more of Brianne's writing at readwave.com/brianne.mcdonald.14.

J.C. Baez

A painter, comic book and storyboard artist and illustrator from Chicago and is a graduate of the city's School Of The Art Institute. He recently completed penciling the Walter Koenig's Things To Come graphic novel published by Bluewater Comics released last December, drew Violin Stories, a comic book for Jon Anderson of the band Yes, and is now developing a graphic novel project with singer Peter Gabriel. Other recent projects include the comic book Makossa, for author Carlton Hargro and storyboards for Star Trek Phase II's episode Kitumba, to be released this year. As a painter, he's been working on a surrealist series of paintings that explore spiritual, social and cultural themes, a series of works based on photos he's taken at concerts in which try to capture the energy of a live performance, and a series of paintings of Jesus in an expressionist manner in a way that updates religious iconography in a modern way. More information on J.C.Baez can be found on his sites jcbaez.daportfolio.com and jcbaezillustration.daportfolio.com and at ArtByStudios.com.

Kara Hamilton

Born in Dayton, Ohio in 1989. At the age of nine, she began experimenting with photography on a family road trip in the Southwest. She graduated from Northern Arizona University in 2011 with a Bachelor of Fine Arts. She has exhibited work throughout Flagstaff, Arizona and received the Northern Arizona University Moller Scholarship for Artistic Achievement in 2010 and 2011. She currently resides in Chicago, Illinois, where she works as a graphic designer. Recent accomplishments include: Receiving a Juror's award in October, 2013 for her mixed-media light boxes at the Studio 659 'Artistic License' show in Whiting, Indiana, Winning the album cover art competition for local Chicago band, OSHWA, and Exhibiting photography in the upcoming December 21, 2013 publication from the Raison d'Être Collective entitled 'What is Your Reason for Being?' See more about Kara at karahamiltonart.com.

Celebrating Diversity Of Talent

Ann Kendall

A writer in Seattle, Washington focusing on architecture, art and human services through grant writing, impact measurements and creative writing. Working with local non-profits, her work often highlights the difficulties faced by communities in need while highlighting the impact high quality human services can have in creating positive change. In her architectural writings she works to bring clarity to complicated and complex ideas that are easily understood; she also currently writes reviews of artistic programs receiving grant funding through her local county. Her creative work has appeared in Faith & Form Magazine. In her spare time she is editing a book on running for her beloved trainer and is participating in NaNoWriMo 2013. See more about Ann at annkendall.com.

Maureen Sebek

It is in the beautiful diamond of creativity that Maureen finds the breathtaking beauty of the Master Artist, the God of All Creativity. As a writer, it is one of the great privileges of her life to celebrate Him in His passionate, endless pursuit of you and me. As a woman, a mother of four grown kids and a former foster parent of twelve foster children over the years, Maureen is well acquainted with the issues that concern women. Her writing focuses on helping women discover God on their journey when they least expect to find Him, loving them, healing them, calling them forward. Follow Maureen on her blog at maureencarrollsebek.blogspot.com.

Rob Tolzien

Born and raised in Chicago, is beginning to get back into the writing game after some recent unique life experiences. He spends much of his time working in the local Chicago theatres as a stagehand, basically being a glorified furniture mover. Outside of work, he spends his time working as a boudoir/pin up photographer and writing short works that either inspire or depress. See more about Rob's photography at RTPhotoWerks.com.

Stephen Thom

A literary artist, from Edinburgh, Scotland, originally from Cambridge in the Highlands. Writing was an old hobby of his that he recently started to indulge in again. See his more of his writings at readwave.com/stephen.thom.505. Stephen is also a musician in an alt folk band named Dante. See more about his band at abadgeoffriendship.com/projects/dante.

Contributors

www.jordanebrooks-com.webs.com

Jordan Brooks

Born and raised in Kansas, Jordan spent much of his life between Topeka and Lawrence city. He has been influenced by a wide variety of work ranging from classical to comic book greats from the 90's. Following his mother, he picked up a pencil at the age 3 and never stopped! But art hasn't always been so clear for him. A once raw source of creativity, has now found guidance as an aspiring student illustrator enrolled in Academy of Art of San Francisco. Gaining confidence, Jordan launched his own creative platform. His website allows him to display his own mix of the academic design, with modern, conceptual and provocative thought drive. The website has also captured National and International attention. Now in 2013, Jordan made a strong impression in New York City during Art fair month. He has been inspired by massive feedback from his first International Group (Power of Perception) exhibition in Historical Harlem, New York city. Jordan's work focuses on the concept of social awareness and overriding power of social media on our environment. His work aims to remind people of their inherent humanity. See more of Jordan at jordanebrooks-com.webs.com as well as at society6.com/JordanBrooks.

Matt Haydu

Matty (23), comes to you from a small town in New England. He spends his days appreciating the simple things in life and his nights wasting away in the studies of astrophysics, anthropology, philosophy, and all breeds of scientific wonder. He owns a science-niche clothing brand called Venus Fallen and is employed by an aerospace company, Sikorsky Aircraft, as an IFM administrator. He aims to inspire progressive thinkers by blending outer space, science and futurism into one sustainable culture. Living in a world where most people follow the norm makes it difficult for those to step out of comfort zones and enter truth and individuality. He writes so that he can connect with others emotionally, positively and creatively on a level that is thought provoking and awe inspiring. Check out his Venus Fallen clothing brand at vf.merchnow.com.

Juliane von Kunhardt

Juliane von Kunhardt is a qualified designer, children portraitist and printmaker from Cologne, Germany. She and her husband raised 4 kids, generations of dogs, cats and chickens in her 200 year old horse carriage mansion. The love to her chickens and dogs led her into a deeper involvement about animal protection. Inspired by the book *Eating Animals* by Jonathan S. Foer, led her to a solo show in Evanston, about food processing, farm factories and eating behavior. Juliane has participated at other printmaking and solo shows after moving to the Chicagoland area. She received a first prize award in the show "Distortion" at the Arterie Fine Arts Gallery, which will host her upcoming solo show January 26th to February 1st 2014. See more about Juliane and her visual art at julesart.org and facebook.com/julesartdotorg.

Leemour Pelli

An artist living and working in New York City, Leemour is a graduate of the School of Visual Arts (B.F.A., painting), Hunter College (Master of Arts degree in Art History) and the Hebrew University of Jerusalem (B.A. in English Literature). She has also studied at the Bezalel Academy of Art in Jerusalem, the Ecole Nationale Superieure des Beaux-Arts, in Paris and at Cornell University. In 2008, the artist had her first solo exhibition at the Daneyal Mahmood Gallery in New York. Her other recent solo exhibitions include two at the Annina Nosei Gallery in New York in 2004 and 2005, and at the Art Gallery of the University of Central Florida in Orlando in 2003. The University published a catalogue and produced a mini documentary about the artist and her work. Pelli's recent exhibitions also include the Robert Fontaine Gallery in Miami, (whom she is currently represented by), Kinz Tillou and Feigen Gallery, and the Paul Rodgers Gallery in New York, the Whitney Museum of American Art at Champion, Connecticut, PS1 Institute of Contemporary Art, Long Island City, Spaces Contemporary Art Center in Ohio, and the Artcore Gallery in Toronto. Her work has been reviewed in ArtForum (2008), Art News, The New York Times, New York Arts Magazine, Tema Celeste, and The Globe and Mail, among other publications.

Lottie Krol

Lottie Krol is an ovarian cancer survivor that has battled the disease numerous times, where now it has become her lifestyle. Cancer has changed her life and taught her how loved she really was. She believes her journey with cancer is the life she is destined to live as she struggles to make sense of it. This journey has brought her to serve and give back by devoting her time to children by teaching Sunday School and running a Crocheting Ministry that provides blankets and other hand-made items to charity. Her ministry can be found at facebook.com/thecrochetingministryclub. Follow Lottie as she writes about her journey at her blog Enjoying The Journey: Cancer As A Lifestyle at lottiekrol.blogspot.com.

EzzyPezzy

EzzyPezzy is a London based Visual Artist who is transfixed by patterns and mesmerised by colour. A lot of her work is either a combination of fine line and marker pen or acrylic and spray paint on canvas. She also works with screen printing and dyeing too. You can find her at facebook.com/ezzypezzyart or on twitter/instagram @ezzypezzyart.

Ben Hardy

Ben Hardy is a keen amateur wine maker and part time writer living in Leeds, England. His wine making exploits can be read in his book, Ben's Adventures in Wine Making, published by the Good Life Press, and on his blog, bensadventuresinwinemaking.blogspot.com. When he is not making wine, Ben can often be found playing the bassoon around Yorkshire (once in a swimming pool) and, under protest, he makes his living as a property lawyer.

Melody Croft

Even though Melody has drawn since childhood, she never thought of herself as an artist until she was 32 years old. About this time she was reading a number of self-help books, one of which recommended watercolor painting as good therapy for self-esteem. She thought, since she could draw, maybe she could try it: what could she lose? After buying a watercolor book and the necessary supplies, she began teaching herself to paint. She paints primarily in oil on canvas now, but also works in collage. Her paintings have simplicity of design, the vibrancy in color, and the surface texture that she loves in the paintings of Amedeo Modigliani.

Her portrait, conceptual and genre paintings, examine the status quo and social norms of modern life. She paints untraditional realistic narratives that invite viewers to observe and consider the psychological, sociological, or emotional complexities of race, gender, age and culture. When she paints, the creative process envelopes her like the threads of a cocoon and allows a safe place to develop emotionally, psychologically and spiritually, much like a cocoon provides a safe place for a caterpillar to transform. To see more of Melody, visit her website at melodycroft.com.

Nithya Narayanan

Nithya Narayanan is a young writer with a passion for the art from Auckland, New Zealand. She believes writing is an integral part of creativity and innovation, and hopes to later share her views with others by promoting creative writing both within New Zealand and internationally, in addition to becoming a published author. She is currently editing and compiling a range of her original poems for submission to Poetry NZ literary magazine and her long-term goal is to have an anthology published by boutique publishing house

Seraph Press based in Wellington. Nithya is also a musician and a self-termed philosopher. See more about Nithya at kiwiwrite.weebly.com.

Imani Sims

Imani Sims is a Seattle native who spun her first performance poem at the age of fourteen. Since then, she has developed an infinitely rippling love for poetry in all of its forms. She believes in the healing power of words and the transformational nuance of the human story. Imani is the founder of Split Six Productions, splitsix.com, an interdisciplinary art production company that works towards connecting artists and putting their stories on stage. Her book *Twisted Oak* is available on Requiem Press. She is currently pursuing her PhD in Transformational Studies at the California Institute of Integral Studies and finalizing her third chapbook for release December 17th, 2013.

Jeri Fredrickson

Jeri Frederickson is a theatre artist in Chicago. She reads scripts over coffee, stage manages and directs late into the night, and has long chats with her cat about poetry. She currently literary manager for Cube, Seanachai Theatre and Artemisia. Recent publication credits include "The Deflation of Love" in Vine Leaves Literary Journal #3 July 2012 and print The Best of Vine Leaves 2012, "Single Cherry Blossom" in Vine Leaves Journal #06 April 2013 and forthcoming in print The Best of Vine Leaves 2013.

Zeta Sin

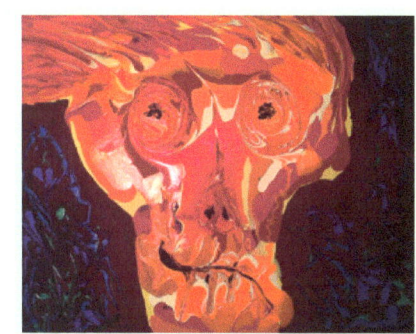

Artistic roots started in sketching around 7th grade, where he received positive feedback from his teachers. This convinced him to continue sketching for many years after and has since invented new ideas for tools, electronics and more. Sketching
allowed Zeta to focus on his ideas which fueled a pursuance of an engineering degree. Eventually, the blacks and various shades of grey to white grew boring to him and decided to take up painting, in terms of the abstract. He found traditional abstract to be too out of form and has developed a few paintings that utilizes his own technique that focuses on blends of colors and several different mediums. For details on purchasing Zeta's Art see artwanted.com/artist..

Kat Lahr

Kat Lahr is Founder and Creative Director for *Thought Collection Publishing*. She enjoys collaborating with other literary and visual artists to collectively bring wisdom, creativity and social change to the world. Kat currently holds an MBA, is an Adjunct Professor, Yogite, Home Winemaker, Mom, and Wife.. www.linkedin.com/in/kathylahr

Thought Collection Publishing partners with artists all over the world to share in diversity of thought and talent.

Making A Difference

coachart

To help bring awareness to and support positive social change around the world, we interview nonprofit organizations to learn more about their goals and impacts. Our community of readers and artists then vote on which organization should receive 10% from every sale of this Journal issue. An overwhelming 80% of the vote went to *CoachArt.*

The creative process involved in expressing one's self artistically can help enhance the well-being of the artist and anyone else involved. That's why people all over are dedicating their careers to Art Therapy, while others are dedicating their time and talents for the same purpose by volunteering. Communities have been using the arts as a way to express, communicate and heal, for all of humanity.

In learning more about Art Therapy, we came across *CoachArt*, an amazing social change organization whose mission is to improve the quality of life for children in Los Angeles and the San Francisco Bay Area with chronic and life threatening illnesses and their siblings, by providing free lessons in the arts and athletics. They rely on volunteer mentors who are matched with patients for lessons that offer creative outlets, such as a distraction from pain, isolation and other ailments often associated with chronic illnesses. The organization's guiding principle is to enhance the lives of chronically ill youth by tapping into the resources from the coaching community. Volunteers from fields such as music, dance, theater, writing and sports, help bring this vision to a reality.

Thought Collection Publishing and the *Thought Notebook* Community, is looking forward to supporting *CoachArt* and their participation in the Art of Improving Lives. See the entire interview at www.thoughtnotebook.org/thoughtful-project.

Donors make a difference. Consider a donation to *CoachArt* at coachart.org/donate.

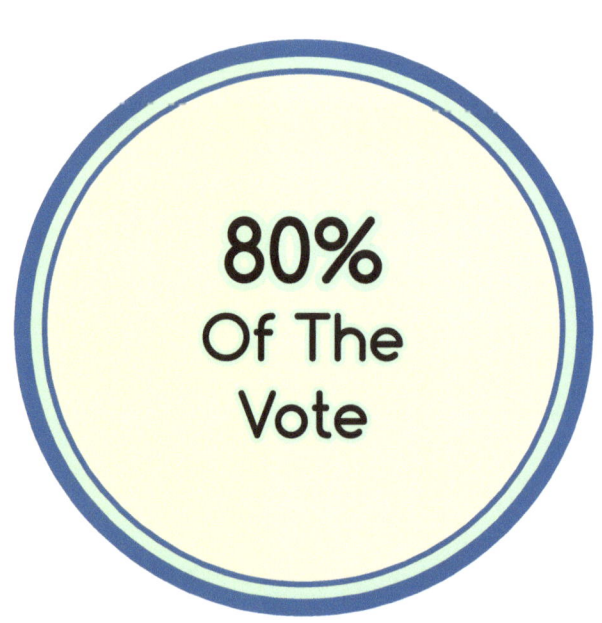

80% Of The Vote

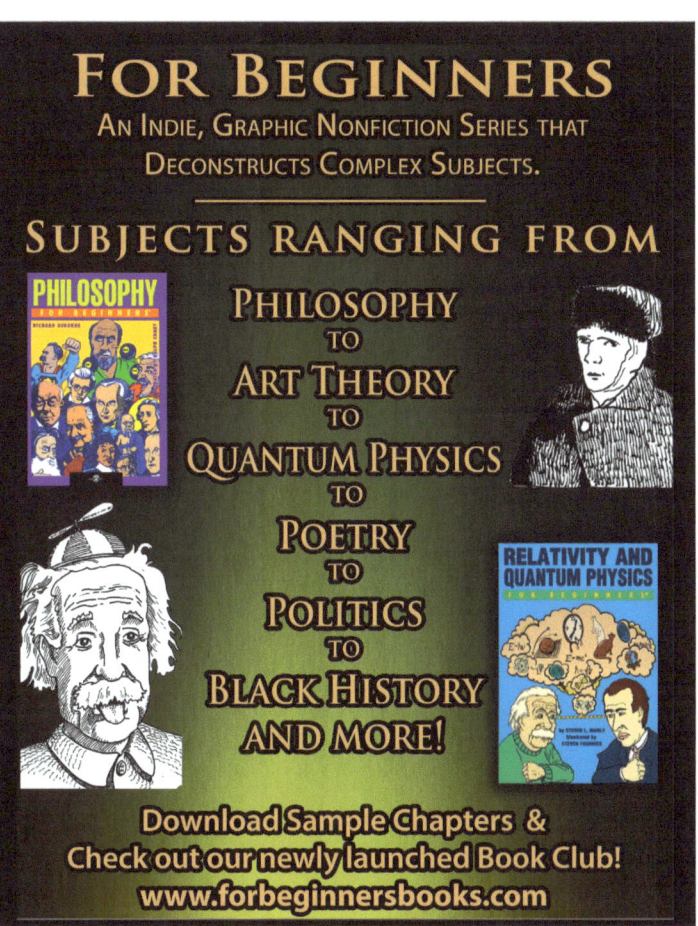

Take The Pledge

Commit to making sustainable personal changes, and collectively we can make a difference in society.

Visit thoughtnotebook.org/pledge to **Take The Pledge Now!**

Webzine Community & Journal

30 DAYS... THOUGHT SERIES COLUMN

We challenge authors to write consecutively for 30 days on a specific area of study or expertise. The first 3-5 days or chapters of their respective manuscripts in our 30 Days... book series is posted to our webzine community. Stay tuned to the column for our first set of writers who took up the challenge.

www. thoughtnotebook.org/30-days

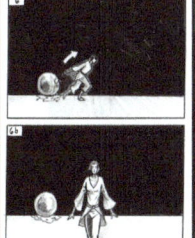
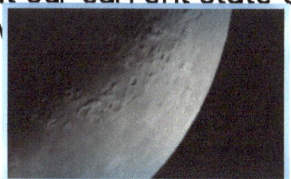

WWW.THOUGHTCOLLECTION.ORG

WWW.THOUGHTNOTEBOOK.ORG

The **HUMAN THOUGHT PROJECT**™ for
Thought Collection Publishing

Publishing For Social Change